5

Tricky Business

GLENN KINSEY

Photography by Katie Vandyck

Illustrations by Steve Carey

BBC BOOKS

Dedicated to Mum, Dad and Suzanne –
the most magical people in the world.

The publishers would like to thank the following people for their
kind help and co-operation in producing this book:

Stacey Lee,
Stacey's Magic Palace,
44 Museum Street,
London,
WC1A 1LY.
for photographic props

Joe Wright,
The White Horse,
94 Brixton Hill,
London,
SW2.
for allowing us to use his
public house for photography

White rabbits hired from:
Nicky Barrass,
A1 Animals,
Plaistow Green Farm,
Winkfield,
Berkshire.

Published by BBC Books,
A division of BBC Enterprises Ltd
Woodlands, 80 Wood Lane, London W12 0TT

First published 1990
© Glenn Kinsey 1990
ISBN 0 563 20923 2

Typeset in Helvetica
by Ace Filmsetting Ltd, Frome
Colour separations by Technik Ltd, Berkhamsted
Printed and bound in Great Britain
by Richard Clay Ltd, Norwich
Jacket printed by Belmont Press Ltd, Northampton

Photography © Katie Vandyck 1990
Illustrations © Steve Carey 1990

CONTENTS

SO, WHO'S GLENN KINSEY?

I want to do a comedy series based in a Magic Shop – plenty of scope for visual humour, great characters, good plot-lines and masses of magic! So far so good. The idea is born – now, I need a magic advisor. I don't want the old image of frilly shirts and glamour assistants. I want new ideas and I want to make it look exciting and relevant to the audience I serve. I read magic books galore, I consult the Magic Circle and then, one day, a colleague recommends I meet a young magician, Glenn Kinsey . . .

The moment I met Glenn, I realised I'd seen him before. I'd auditioned him for a TV talent show I was producing – he was brilliant but too old! The age limit was 13, and he was 14. The thing that impressed me greatly about him then, and the same applies even more now, is that his act is very *entertaining*; it was not the 'Aren't I clever' type of magic presentation, it was real entertainment; his chat was funny and his approach was refreshingly original.

I talked to him about my ideas for a new-look magic series. He was enthusiastic. Glenn is a great enthusiast. I sensed he was caught by the idea and he was immediately suggesting tricks and guests. It was a good meeting. I booked him at once.

It was a risk of course. He'd never 'advised' before and he was only 18! But, as his first solo performance on a stage was at the age of four, he'd had a head start! At 11 he was already winning awards, including 'Butlin's Junior Star Trail'. He did his first television appearance at the age of 13, and more followed. By the age of 15 he was being booked to appear in theatres and major hotels and he was a finalist in the 'Young Magician of the Year'.

Despite this, Glenn wisely kept his schoolwork going and, at 16, he passed an incredible 12 'O' Levels! Little wonder then, that at the same age he was appointed Entertainments Manager for one of Blackpool's largest hotel companies. At 17 he established several seasonal retail outlets in Blackpool and presented over 200 cabaret and children's shows. When he turned 18 he went to Spain and became Entertainments Director for a prominent group of hotels and developed an entertainments programme which gave them record profits.

Hundreds of cabaret, theatre and TV shows later, Glenn has developed a unique comedy magic act which won for him a TV talent show at the age of 19. 'I don't think I've ever heard an act get so many laughs,' said panellist and famous comedian Frank Carson.

Since working on the first series of 'Tricky Business', other BBC programmes have booked Glenn as their magic advisor. Equally, his on-screen, on-stage presence is in continual demand.

Glenn has packed so much into his life already; it is an inspiration to us all. At the time of writing, Glenn is still 19 – he must be the youngest 'expert' in the business! I know Glenn has ambitions outside the world of magic, such as hosting his own unusual chat show. Having seen some of Glenn's television presentation work already, Terry Wogan had better watch out – 'Glenn's about!'

Christopher Pilkington
Executive Producer, Children's BBC Television

INTRODUCTION

Magic's been good to me. It's opened dozens of doors, created countless friendships and loaded my life with laughter. And it can do the same for you, too. How? Well, contrary to popular opinion, you don't need a power-packed personality, acrobatic fingers and a velvet bow tie to do magic.

But what you do need is an overwhelming desire to entertain people. Armed with that and this book, you'll develop a priceless skill which you can call upon and use for the rest of your life. You'll fascinate and intrigue wherever you go. People will warm to you. Friends will be made easily. And you'll be able to feel that wonderful sensation of captivating and entertaining an audience – whether you're doing a trick at a party, or at the Palladium.

Remember that what you say while doing your magic is important. For many of the tricks I've suggested some ideas. These are for guidance only – chop and change the patter to suit your personality.

So, I won't keep you any longer. Dive into this book and watch *your* life change into a 'Tricky Business' . . . just like magic!

COME A LITTLE CLOSER

No, even closer still, because here are some 'close-up' tricks – magic which happens right under the spectators' noses. So don't do them in front of anyone with a cold . . . .

THE HAUNTED KEY

This is creepy! A large key eerily turns over on your hand. Are there ghosts at work? No, they're not. In fact, this trick is so simple you wouldn't believe it. I didn't. I remember when a magician called Tony Clinning first showed me this – I was baffled for weeks.

HOW IT'S DONE

Down to the trick. Get hold of a large key and place it on your hand as in the photograph. Pretend to pluck a hair from your head and wind it around the end of the key. Now, tilt your hand ever so slowly and you'll find the key will turn over. At the same time, pretend to be pulling it with the thread. Don't give the game away by jerking your palm, and make sure you time the action of pulling the thread correctly. If you follow the instructions you'll have a miracle in your pocket. Oh, and you'll be able to get into your house with it . . . .

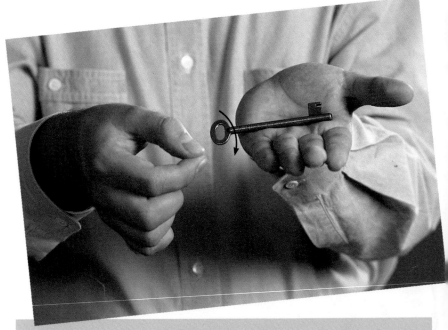

WHAT YOU COULD SAY

'Watch this, I'll produce a rabbit before your very eyes.' (Pluck a pretend hair from your head and hold it up). 'There you are . . . it's not a rabbit, it's a hare . . . hair? Get it? Oh never mind.' (An awful joke). 'This is how Houdini used to escape.' (Place key on hand). 'He'd take a magic hair, wind it around the key and do this . . .' (Turn key over). 'Just like magic!'

THE DOUBLE-SIDED KNIFE WITH SIX SIDES

You show a knife with bits of tissue paper stuck to it. You wipe them off but, wonder of wonders, they jump back. The kid's a miracle worker!

HOW IT'S DONE

This is a good one for the dinner table – all you need is a knife and a paper hanky or napkin. Tear four small pieces off the hanky or napkin. They should all be about the same size. Stick two on each side of the knife by wetting them with your tongue. Hold the knife in your right hand as in 1 . Turn the hand over and up, but as you do this rotate the knife with your thumb and forefinger, as in 2 . It looks as if you are showing both sides of the knife but, being the sneaky little devil that you are, you've only shown one side. Reverse the movements to bring the knife back to the position shown in **1**. Magicians call this 'the paddle move' – done properly, the whole thing is very convincing. Slide one piece of tissue off with the thumb of your left hand. Do the move so that it looks as if the piece on the other side has come off too. Repeat this, so that the knife appears to be blank on both sides. Wave your right hand quickly from side to side, rotating the knife with your thumb as you do so. Click the fingers of your left hand. The tissue appears to have magically jumped back onto the knife. Show the knife on both sides by means of the 'paddle move', and a miracle has been accomplished. Wipe the blade with a cloth to remove the tissue so that everything can be examined. It's a good trick, isn't it?

WHAT YOU COULD SAY

'A trick with a knife and a tissue . . . bless you! There's two bits on this side and two bits on this side . . . but if I slide this piece off' (slide a piece of tissue off the knife) '. . . the one on the other side jumps off too! I'll do it again . . . slide this piece off, and the other jumps off too! That leaves us with a knife and no tissue. Who wants to see the trick again? Then I just click my fingers and we're back where we started with two on this side, and two on this side.'

THE TORN AND RESTORED CIGARETTE PAPER

You hold a piece of cigarette paper (you know, the stuff they use for those roll-your-own cigarettes) in your hands. There's clearly nothing else there apart from the paper. You tear it into tiny pieces and roll them into a ball. But when you open out the ball the paper is seen to be completely restored – and there's absolutely nothing else in your hands. As we say in Lancashire, 'They'll be gobsmacked!'

HOW IT'S DONE

You'll need a packet of cigarette papers, but for goodness' sake, don't smoke – your health will suffer. Roll one of the papers up into a ball. Hide it behind a protruding paper from the packet as shown in 1 . You're all set. Take the protruding paper from the packet, along with the hidden ball of paper. Conceal the hidden ball behind the paper with your right thumb as in 2 . This is easy because the ball is so small. Tear the paper up into little pieces, taking care to keep the paper ball hidden between the right thumb and forefinger. Roll the torn pieces into a ball with your left fingertips. Use your right hand to help 'press' the pieces together as in 3 . As you're doing this, bring the 'restored' ball into view and hide the torn pieces between your left forefinger and thumb. Now, begin to pick at the 'restored' ball as you try to open it out. Touch

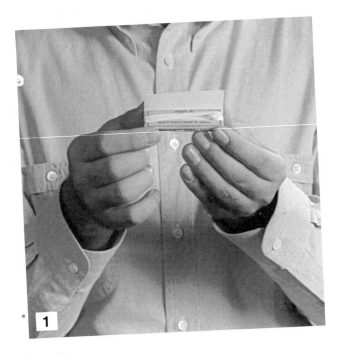

1

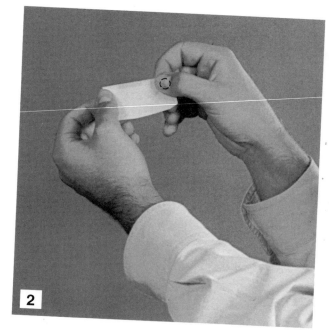

2

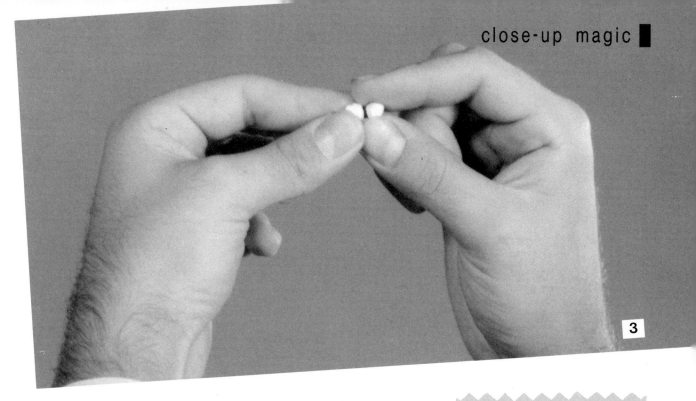

3

your left forefinger and thumb to your lips and tongue, as if wetting them to help you open out the paper. At this point let the bits of rolled up paper drop into your mouth. Now that's a sneaky move if ever I saw one! It should only take a fraction of a second to do this. Conceal it behind your lip. Because it's so small you'll still be able to talk with it in your mouth and you can take it out later when no-one's watching. All that's left now is to open out the ball, showing the paper to be completely in one piece. A nice touch is to gently blow the paper into the air from your fingertips. This will show the audience that there's nothing wrong with the paper.

CHUCKLE BOX

When you ask someone their name: 'What's your name? That's my dog's name! Are you house trained too?'

If you drop something, say this as you bend to pick it up: 'I haven't been feeling very well lately, but I'm picking up.'

WHAT YOU COULD SAY

'I'm going to show you the illusion of the torn and restored cigarette paper. It's called an illusion because *I never actually tear the paper at all.*' (Begin tearing). 'You know, people actually think that I'm tearing the paper. Some say they can even *hear* me tearing the paper into little pieces.' (Keep tearing then show the separate pieces). 'Some *even* say that they can actually *see* separate pieces of paper! But it's all an illusion.' (Roll the paper into a ball). 'And here they are, completely restored! You don't believe me? I'll show you, look. . . .' (Open out the paper, showing it to be in one piece).

MAKING MONEY

So how does a magician make money? By changing pieces of paper into crisp £5 notes!

HOW IT'S DONE

You'll need a £5 note, preferably a brand new one, and a piece of paper which is exactly the same size as the £5, cut from a magazine. Lay the £5 on a table with the queen looking up. Fold it in half as in ⌐1⌐ and then in half again ⌐2⌐. Fold it in half upwards ⌐3⌐ so that it looks something like ⌐4⌐. Do exactly the same with the piece of paper. Stick a couple of small pieces of Blu-Tac to the paper as shown in ⌐5⌐. With me so far? OK, now turn the folded fiver upside down and stick it to the paper with the Blu-Tac ⌐6⌐. Open the paper out and hold it in your left hand as in ⌐7⌐, taking care to keep the £5 folded and hidden by the fingers. Turn your hand over to show both sides, making sure the audience can't see any of the £5. Fold the paper in half ⌐8⌐ and in half again ⌐9⌐. Fold the top half down ⌐10⌐ and then turn the whole lot over, including the £5 as in ⌐11⌐. The audience will see the £5. Open it out, taking care that the folded paper is concealed from view. Finally,

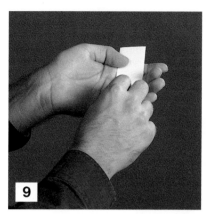

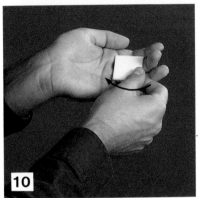

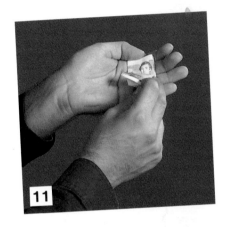

pull the £5 away from the paper so that it breaks free of the Blu-Tac. Keep looking at the £5 as you take it away with your right hand. While you do this, drop your left hand to your side with the paper hidden in your fingers. As you hold the £5 up to the light, casually slip the paper into your pocket and, while it's there, grab your wallet or purse and bring it out, putting the £5 inside. A point to remember – when you're doing the folding and

unfolding, always keep your hands at waist height and tilted towards the audience. If you do this, they will never see the package underneath. And if you keep making money like this,

you'll never need to work again!

WHAT YOU COULD SAY

(Say all this quickly). 'I'll show you how I make money. I take a piece of paper.' (Show both sides). 'Fold it over there, over there, over there. Say the magic word "Alibrontifossifallyfolio" and we have, a £5 note.' (Snap it off the Blu-Tac; hold it up to the light as if checking that it's a real one. Grab your wallet and bring it out). 'Every other show I give £5 away.' (Hold out the £5 to a spectator, then pull it back as he reaches for it). 'But this isn't the other show!'

LET'S PLAY BALL

Spongy balls vanish and reappear in a spectator's hands and finally turn into a cube! Believe me, this is one of the best close-up tricks you'll ever learn.

HOW IT'S DONE

You'll need four balls made from nylon foam bath sponge, each one about 3 cm (1.2 in) in diameter. Make these by cutting squares from the sponge, and then trimming the edges to make balls. While you've got the scissors and sponge out, cut a cube about 4 cm × 4 cm (1.5 in × 1.5 in). You can buy some fabulous sponges from magic shops, made by a man called Albert Goshman. Practise concealing a ball in your hand as in 1 . Just hold it there gently; don't squeeze too tightly, and forget all about it. This is called the 'palm' and it's used throughout the trick to secretly hide a ball in your hand. Put the cube in your right trouser, skirt or jacket pocket. Put the four balls on top. To present the trick, reach into your pocket with your right hand. Palm one of

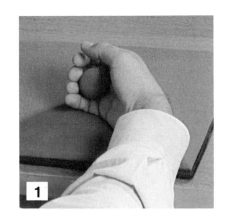

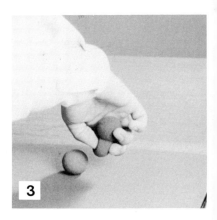

the balls and bring another two out with your fingertips as shown in 2 . Put both balls on the table. With your right hand, pick up the ball on your right hand side and put the ball in your left hand, secretly adding the palmed ball at the same time as in 3 . Take the remaining ball on the table and put this in your pocket. While your

hand is there, grab the other ball and palm them both. Bring your hand out of your pocket and let it hang naturally by your side. Ask a spectator how many balls are in your left hand. Open your left hand to reveal two balls and put them on the table. Repeat the whole thing, this time adding two extra balls to your left hand. Leave the one ball in your pocket this time, and bring your right hand out empty. When you open your left hand, you've got three balls. Now, pick up one of the balls holding it in your right fingers. Put the ball in the centre of your left palm and slowly close your fingers around it. As you do this, move all your right fingers, apart from your forefinger, over the ball. Finally, as you close your left hand completely, stretch your forefinger out and press the ball under your fingers with your right thumb as in 4 . Move your right hand away with the ball hidden behind your fingers, held there by your thumb 5 . That all sounds very complicated, but it should only take a couple of seconds. It looks as if you've put a ball in your left hand. Practise the movements in front of a mirror to get the timing right. Pick up one of the two balls on the table, adding the concealed ball in your right hand. Squeeze these two together – it looks as if you are only holding one ball. Put these into the spectator's hand, and close her hand over them. Put the remaining ball in your right pocket, secretly palming the cube. Open your left hand – there's nothing there! Ask the spectator to open her hand revealing two balls. OK so far? Good. Pick up

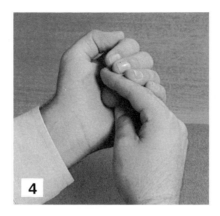

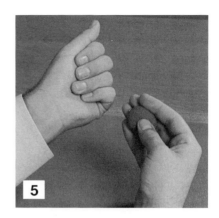

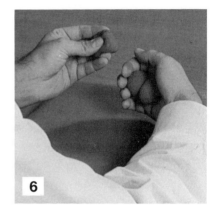

the two balls with your right hand and bend your fingers into your palm. Bring your left hand across and grab the cube, squashing it between the left fingertips. At the same time, bend the balls into the palm position and move your left hand away with the squashed cube, as shown in 6 . *Keep looking at your left hand.* This is called 'misdirection'. Because the cube is squashed up, it will look as if you are clutching the two balls. Put the cube in a spectator's hand, making sure she closes it tightly. Put your right hand into your

pocket, leaving the balls behind and bring out some pretend 'Woofle Dust'. Sprinkle this over the spectator's hand, ask her to open it and, lo and behold, it's a square!

WHAT YOU COULD SAY

'Two balls. One in the hand, one in the pocket. How many here?' ('One') 'Two! I'll start again . . . one in the hand, one in the pocket . . . how many here?' ('One' or 'Two') 'Three! One in my hand, one in your hand, one in my pocket. Open your hand . . . two! Two in your hand, how many have you got? I thought you looked a bit square!'

COIN CONNIVERY

Stop counting all that money! Instead, grab a few coins, wander through the following pages, and you'll always have a miracle in your pocket – unless you spend it!

HOW TO MAKE A COIN DISAPPEAR – AND FIND IT IN SOMEONE'S EAR

The most magical thing that ever happened to me was when I was seven years old. A magician made a coin disappear and then produced it from behind my ear. It puzzled me for years afterwards. I now regularly perplex my nephew, Adam, with the same trick.

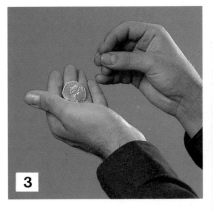

HOW IT'S DONE

Magicians often use a move called 'The French Drop'. Here is my version of it. Start with the coin held in your left hand as in 1 . Bring your right hand across, putting your thumb behind the coin, your fingers in front 2 . Without making any notice-

able movement of the left hand, let the coin drop into your fingers. Press your right thumb and fingers together as if holding the coin, and move them away as in 3 . *Keep looking at the right hand!* Casually drop your left hand down by your side, gently gripping

the coin with the joints of your fingers. Blow on your right hand and open it slowly, showing that the coin has disappeared. Now, reach up behind someone's ear with your left hand and, pushing the coin up to your fingertips, let it make contact with the person's ear as you pull your hand away from their head. Display the coin at the tips of your fingers. I can assure you, this is the most magical thing in the world to a small child. Try it.

'THERE'S A HOLE IN MY HAND, DEAR AUDIENCE, DEAR AUDIENCE . . .'

A coin passes right through the back of your hand. And you can't even see the hole!

HOW IT'S DONE

Hold the coin in your right hand above your clenched fist as in 1 . Rub the coin across the back of your hand as if trying to push it through. As you do this, let the coin slide up behind the

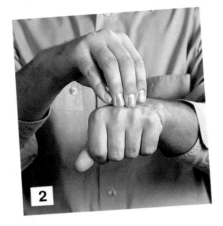

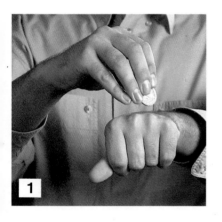

look directly at the spectators, *not at your hands!* Now all you have to do is pretend to push the coin through your hand as in 2. Show your right hand is empty, then open your left hand to display the coin.

fingers of your right hand 2 . Stop, as if the trick's worked, and turn your left hand upwards, looking surprised when you see there's nothing there. Now for the crucial bit. As you say something like, 'Ooops! That didn't work, I'll try again,' you begin to turn your left

hand back over. As this happens, secretly let the coin drop from your right fingertips into the left hand 3 . Keep turning the left hand over, forming it back into a fist. But you must add one more element to all this – misdirection. So as you're doing the sneaky moves,

CHUCKLE BOX

When someone asks you how a trick is done: 'How's it done? Well, can you keep a secret? Yes? So can I!'

THE COINS AND GLASS THROUGH A TABLE

1

Three coins pass through a solid table top – then, in full view, a glass does the same thing! Another one that'll simply blow 'em away!

HOW IT'S DONE

Four coins are needed, a sheet of newspaper and a glass tumbler. Start with the four coins held in your right hand as in 1 , making sure that the coin nearest your fingertips is gripped between the joints of your middle fingers. Toss three coins into your left hand, secretly keeping the end coin gripped by the joints of your right hand. Magicians call this the 'finger palm' 2 . Close your left hand over the three coins – the audience will think your left hand holds four coins. Put your right hand under the table and slap your left hand palm downwards onto the table top. Turn your left hand slowly over, to reveal three coins. Bring your right hand

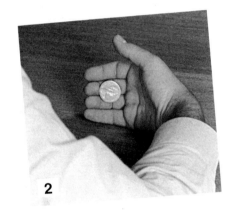

2

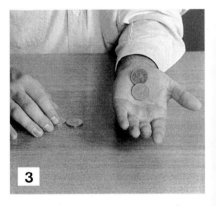

3

out from under the table displaying the coin, showing that it has, apparently, passed through the table. As the thunderous applause subsides (!), put the coin held in your right hand onto the table. Pick up the other three coins and, as before, throw them into your left hand, keeping one behind in the right. Pick the remaining coin up from the table, keeping the finger palmed coin hidden. Slam your left hand down onto the table again,

and show that the second coin has gone through the table. Put the two coins back into your left hand, in the position shown in 3 . Turn your hand over and close it. You should find your fingers are just touching one coin as in 4 . Pick up the two remaining coins with your right hand and hold them up. As you do this, move your left hand backwards, letting the coin drop from outside your fist onto your lap. Put your right hand under the table, picking up the other coin from your lap. Following me so far? Slam your left hand onto the table again and show that a third coin has passed through. Say that the last coin is the most difficult, so you must cover it with the glass. Wrap a sheet of newspaper around the glass, so that its shape can still be seen. Put it over the one coin on the table, and command the coin to go. Triumphantly lift up the glass and look surprised when you see that the coin hasn't gone. Repeat this again, but this time, lift up the glass and move it backwards. Keep moving it towards the edge of the table and let the glass fall onto your lap from the news-paper 5 . While this is happening, lean forward

4

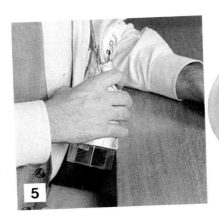

5

and *look at the coin.* The audience will always look where you look, so they won't see you dropping the glass on your lap. The paper retains the shape of the glass, so everyone will think it's still there. Put this paper 'shell' over the coin, making a 'magical' gesture with your hand. Slam your hand down on top of the paper, crushing it flat. Produce the glass from under the table. It's a good idea to put a napkin over your lap, so that a coin doesn't accidentally fall through your legs and onto the floor.

WHAT YOU COULD SAY

'A trick with four coins, two hands . . . and a lot of nerve! Every table has a soft spot . . . there's one just here.' (You slap your left palm downwards onto the table top). 'I'll try that again . . . coin number two!' (Slam your left hand down onto the table again). 'Two coins left.' (Put the two coins back into your hand). 'Coin number 3!' (Slam your left hand onto the table again). 'The hardest coin is the last one. I'll cover it with the glass. And the coin has gone through the . . . . Oh, dear. I'll try again . . . still not worked; I may have missed the soft spot.' (Move the coin onto the 'soft spot', simultaneously dropping the glass onto your lap). 'And the coin has *gone!*' (Produce the glass slowly from beneath the table. Look puzzled). 'How *did I do that*? Shall I show you a card trick instead?'

THAT'S AMAZING!

This will blow their minds! A marked coin disappears from inside a glass – and is found inside a little bag, which is inside a matchbox, which is inside another matchbox – and the whole thing is sealed with rubber bands! Now *that's amazing!*

HOW IT'S DONE

You'll need a handkerchief, a piece of thread, sticky labels, two matchboxes (one smaller than the other), some rubber bands, a little cloth bag which fits inside the smaller matchbox, a glass, a ruler and a piece of scrap tin, about 5 cm × 10 cm (2 in × 4 in), cut from a can. You need the tin for making a chute to drop the coin down. The best way to cut the tin is by removing the top and bottom from a can and then flattening the sides out before cutting out the shape. Be very careful you don't hurt yourself, as the fewer number of fingers you have the harder the trick is to perform. Bend the tin around the ruler as in  to make a chute ❷. Make sure the coin will slide down it without getting stuck. Put the chute inside the bag and secure the top of the bag with a rubber band ❸. Slip this into the smaller matchbox with the chute protruding. Wrap some bands lengthways around the box ❹. Put this box into the larger one, with the chute protruding through the drawer. Wrap some more bands around the box as in ❺. Put all this into your jacket pocket. Oh, and I almost forgot, you'll need to prepare the handkerchief as in ❻, attaching the thread to the centre of the hanky. Stick a 5p piece to the other end of the thread with some Sellotape. Don't make the thread too long – the 5p should be about 2.5

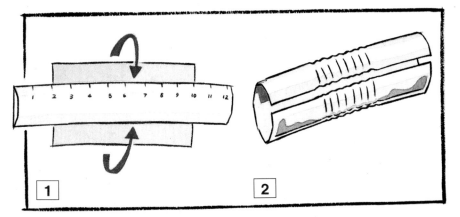

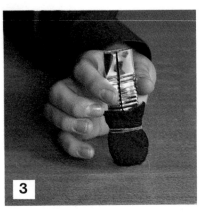

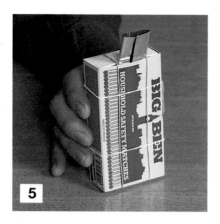

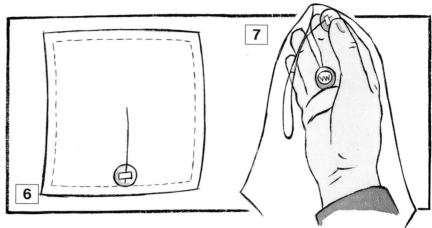

cm (1 in) away from the edge of the hanky. We're all set! Borrow a small coin, for example, a 5p piece. Stick a label onto it. Ask a spectator to write his initials onto the label. Grab the hanky and hold it by its centre in your left hand. Holding the marked coin in your right fingertips, put it under the hanky. As you do this, let the coin fall into your fingers and grab the coin on the thread, pushing it up under the hanky as shown in 7 . Let a spectator hold the 'thread coin' through the hanky. With the marked coin concealed in your fingers, put your hand in your pocket, dropping the coin down the chute. Pull the chute away from the boxes and bring them out, leaving the chute behind. The rubber bands will keep the boxes closed. Put the box on the table. Ask the spectator to hold the hanky over the glass and let go of the coin, allowing it to fall into the glass. He will think that it's the marked coin that he hears falling into the glass. In actual fact, it's the coin on the thread. Clever! Whip the hanky up and away from the glass, and ask the spectator to take his coin out. You'll get some puzzled looks as he finds there's nothing there. Put the hanky away and ask the spectator to open the box on the table. After removing the bands, opening the boxes and opening the cloth bag, he'll find his 5p piece, with his initials, inside it.

WHAT YOU COULD SAY

'My first trick is impossible – so now for my second trick. I'd like to borrow a 5p piece.' (Borrow a 5p piece, stick a label on it, and ask someone to write his initial on the label). 'Here's a felt pen . . . I know because I just "felt" it!' (Groan). 'Sign your initials across the label so you'll know the coin if . . . I mean, *when*, you see it again.' 'I'll put it under this hanky. Could you hold onto it please? This is my insurance box. Drop the coin into this glass. Now take out the 5p from the glass. It's not there? Oh . . . er . . . well, that's the end of that trick! Oh! I almost forgot – my insurance box. Take the rubber bands off and open the box. Tell everyone what you find . . . another box! Take off the bands. What's inside? A bag! Open the bag and take out what's inside. A 5p piece? If they're your initials shout "Amazing!".'

52 BITS OF CARDBOARD

Just what *is* so intriguing about 52 bits of cardboard? Well, I'm not quite sure. But I *am* sure that 'Card Magic' is extremely popular. Buy yourself a good quality pack of cards. You'll find them a lot easier to handle – a poor quality pack is about as much use as a handbrake in a canoe!

''ERE! MIX THESE UP WILL YOU.'

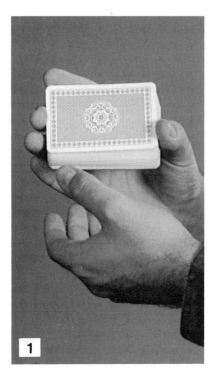

Do you know how to shuffle a pack of cards? Well, I'll show you. This is called the 'overhand shuffle'. Hold the pack in your right hand as in 1 . Draw some cards off with your left thumb and let them fall into your left hand 2 . Move your right hand up and down, pulling more cards off with your left thumb each time 3 . Do this until all the cards are in your left hand. Keep practising and, after a while, you'll be able to do it quickly and without hesitation.

FALSE ACCOUNTING

My, this is strange. After just showing you how to shuffle a pack, I'm going to show you how *not* to shuffle a pack! 'Is Glenn playing with a full deck?' I hear you ask. Actually, this is very handy. It looks as if you're shuffling a pack, but you're not. If you see what I mean. Hold the pack as in 1 for the 'overhand shuffle'. Draw off about half the pack with your left thumb. Then let the rest of the pack fall on top of the cards in your left hand. Pick the pack up in your right hand, and repeat the movement. What you're actually doing is continually cutting the pack – and cutting a pack never disturbs its order. To make this convincing, however, it must be done at speed.

THE KEY TO THE PACK

Ask a spectator to choose a card from the pack. While he is looking at this card, memorize the bottom card of your pack. Now, ask him to place his card on top of the pack, and then cut the cards. If you spread the pack out you will automatically know which card is his. How? Look for the card that was originally on the bottom of the pack. To the right of this card will be the spectator's choice. This is called the 'Key Card' principle.

YOU'RE NOT PLAYING WITH A FULL DECK

How would you like to be able to spread the pack towards a spectator, he takes a card, and you automatically know what it is? Follow my instructions and you'll soon be doing this and other miracles. I'm going to show you how to 'stack' a deck. A 'stacked' deck is one that is pre-arranged into a certain order, enabling you to know the location of every single card in the pack. This particular method was originated by a man called Si Stebbins. Each card in the sequence is *three* more than the card before it. For example, if the top card is a four, the next card will be a seven, the next a ten, the next a King (13) and so on. The suits are in a certain order too – Clubs, Hearts, Spades, Diamonds. You can remember this by picturing the word CHaSeD in your mind. 'C' for Clubs, 'H' for Hearts, 'S' for Spades, 'D' for Diamonds. The photograph shows the complete set-up.

If you've followed me so far, you'll know that if the top card is the Ace of Diamonds, the next card would be the Four of Clubs. If it was the King of Spades, the next one would be the Three of Diamonds. With the whole pack set like this you can cut them as many times as you like, or even false shuffle (see page 21) the cards without disturbing the order.

YOUR CARD IS . . .

This trick is based upon the 'stacked' deck. Spread the cards towards a spectator and ask him to choose one. When he's done this, cut the pack at that point putting the bottom section on the top. Now, look at the bottom card of the pack. Don't make it obvious, just glance at it. His card will be three more on in the next suit. To ensure you don't disturb the order, put his chosen card back on top of the pack, and you'll be able to do the trick again.

THE MIDDLE CARD

This is amazing. Ask the spectator to cut the pack as many times as he likes (making sure he cuts it with the bottom half going on the top each time). Glance at the bottom card. The twenty sixth card in the pack will be of the same value and the corresponding suit. Translated into English, this means that if the bottom card is the Four of Spades the middle (26th) card will be the Four of Clubs. If it was the Nine of Diamonds, the middle card would be the Nine of Hearts. Explain that you could not possibly know the middle card in the pack, since the spectator has been cutting the cards, changing the middle card each time. Name it, and then count down 26 cards to prove that you were right. Heh! You're pretty good, aren't you!

MAY THE FORCE BE WITH YOU

How do you make someone take *exactly* the card you want them to take? I'll tell you. The card you want to be chosen (the 'force card') is on top of the pack. Hold the pack in your left hand, and bring your right hand over the top, fingers at the front of the deck, thumbs at the back nearest you as in 1 . Now, pressing against the pack with your right

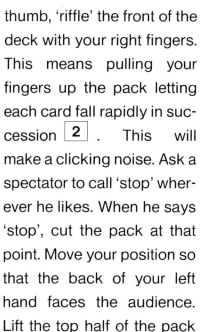

thumb, 'riffle' the front of the deck with your right fingers. This means pulling your fingers up the pack letting each card fall rapidly in succession 2 . This will make a clicking noise. Ask a spectator to call 'stop' wherever he likes. When he says 'stop', cut the pack at that point. Move your position so that the back of your left hand faces the audience. Lift the top half of the pack

away with your right hand. As you do this, hold back the top card by pressing on it lightly with your left fingers 3 . Move your right hand up and away, so that the card held back with your left fingers falls on top of the cards in your left hand. Offer the cards towards a spectator and push off the top card. Congratulations! You've just 'forced' a card.

WHAT YOU COULD SAY

'Sir, as I flick through, shout "stop". Where you stop will be your chosen card.' (Riffle through the pack so quickly that he shouts 'stop' when you've finished). 'No, the idea is, you shout "stop" as I'm flicking through.' (Repeat the action). 'Ready, one, two, three . . .' (On 'three', jerk your hands – he'll shout 'stop'). *'I haven't started!!'* (Riffle through, allowing him to stop at a card). 'We can see that card . . .' (show the bottom card of the pile in your right hand) '. . . so take the next one.' (Push off the top card in your left hand).

HERE IS YOUR CARD. THE NINE ... OR WAS IT THE FIVE?

Take the Nine of Spades from an old pack. Tear it in half as in 1 so that only five Spades are left on the card. Slip this into your pocket, the untorn side uppermost, and with the front of the card facing away from your body. Force the Five of Spades and launch into this . . .

1

WHAT YOU COULD SAY

'I have in my pocket, your card . . . and here it is!' (With this, pull the Nine of Spades into view, but without disclosing that it's torn in half. The audience will soon tell you that it isn't the correct card). 'What do you mean? I promise you, this is your card! It isn't? Well, what was your card? The Five? That's what it is!' (Pull the card out of your pocket). 'There we are, one, two, three, four, five . . . .'

THE INSURANCE POLICY

Draw a duplicate of the force card on a large piece of paper – the bigger the better. Fold this up into a small packet, and on the outside of the packet write 'Insurance Policy'. Have this in your pocket. Force the card on a spectator, then tell him you'll name his card. Call out several cards, none of which are the force card. In desperation say that you'll have to resort to your 'Insurance Policy'. Reach into your pocket and pull out the policy. Open it out to reveal a giant picture of his chosen card. It's simple, but very effective.

THE WORLD'S MOST AMAZING CARD TRICK

Right! Get a load of this! You hand a pack of cards to a spectator. He is asked to deal the cards *face down* into two piles, putting the cards he thinks are red (Hearts and Diamonds) in one pile and the cards he thinks are black (Clubs and Spades) in another. Lo and behold, when the cards are turned over, the reds are in one pile and the blacks are in another!

HOW IT'S DONE

Thought you'd ask that! Deal 23 red cards face down in a pile on the table. on top of this put 24 black cards, then two red cards, a black card, a red card and a black card. Hold the pack face down in your left hand. Turn over the top card (a black one) and put this on the table to your left. Turn over the next card (a red one) and put this to your right. Continue like this until you have dealt seven cards, putting the blacks on the left and the reds on the right as in 1 . As you're doing this, you remark how easy it would be to separate the cards in this fashion. Pick up three of the black cards and insert them one at a time into the top half of the pack (the black section). Do this casu-

ally as if inserting them at random. Pick up two of the red cards inserting these into the bottom half of the pack. You will now have one black card on the table to your left, and a red card to your right. Hand the pack to a spectator and ask him to deal the cards *face down*, putting the cards he thinks to be red on the red 'marker' and the cards he thinks to be black on the black 'marker'. While he does this, count the cards he's dealing silently to

yourself. When he reaches 24, stop him. Take the remaining cards from him. The top card will be black, the rest red. There will be two piles of cards beneath the 'markers' on the table as in 2 . Tell him you're

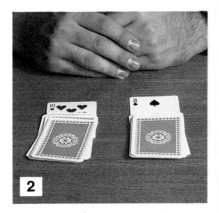

going to change things around. Turn over the top card from the pack in your hand (a black) and put this beneath the red pile. Turn over the next card (a red) and put this beneath the

too busy shaking his head in bewilderment. Here's an extra little touch you can add to the trick which gives it a good ending. Have a Joker inside your top trouser or skirt pocket, back towards the audience. As your assistant hesitates slightly when deciding which pile to put a card on, say 'You're hesitating with that one, I'll put it here'. Don't show the face of the card and tuck it into your pocket. Push it out of view then pull the Joker up, so it protrudes about a third of the way out of your pocket. At the end, show that the card he hesitated on was the Joker.

black pile. Hand the cards back to him and ask him to continue, but this time using the new 'markers' as a guide ③ . When he has dealt all the cards ask him to check the cards in the pile to your left. When he turns them

over he will find that he has guessed correctly, and the blacks are separated from the reds. This is also true of the pile to your right, but the markers are in the wrong places. This is what you

should do. While he's checking the pile on the left, scoop up the right pile. Take out the two markers and throw them onto the table. Then turn over the cards and spread them on the table, showing that the reds are separated from the blacks. The fact that the markers were in the wrong places will not be noticed. He'll be

WHAT YOU COULD SAY

'Sir, if I was to ask you to deal these cards face up, putting the black cards in one pile and the reds in another, you'd find it very easy wouldn't you? But what I'd like you to do is deal them *face down*, putting the cards you think are red here and the cards you think are black here. Let's change things around. This time, put the blacks on this side, and the reds on this side. OK, you have guessed which cards are red and which cards are black. Have a look at this pile, see how you've done. And it's exactly the same over here. The only card you hesitated on was this one, and it's the Joker!'

THE EMBARRASSED CARD

This, I assure you, will blow their brains out! You spread a pack of cards with a blue back design towards a spectator. You ask him to *name* any card. When he does, you turn the pack over and spread them out. One card in the pack has a red back design. When it's removed, it's found to be their chosen card. Wow!

Double Sided tape

HOW IT'S DONE

You'll need some double-sided sticky tape, a red-backed Three of Diamonds, and a blue-backed pack of cards. Cut out a couple of tiny pieces of double-sided tape, about the same size as the small 'Diamonds' on the card. Stick them over the Diamonds, as in the illustration. Take the Three of Diamonds from the blue deck and put this face-up on top of the pack. Put the red-backed Three of Diamonds face up on top of this. Spread the pack face up towards the audience and ask someone to name a card. Find their card and take it out of the pack, taking care not to show its back. Put the card on top of the pack, in other words, on top of the Three of Diamonds. The Three will stick to it.

Take the two cards off the top of the pack and put them face up on the table. Because they are stuck together they look like only one card. Turn the pack over and spread the cards showing that they have blue backs. Now, slowly turn over their chosen card on the table, and watch their mouths drop as they see the red back! Don't worry about

the two cards stuck together. Just handle them confidently, as if they were one card, and no one will suspect a thing. Promise!

◆   ◆   ◆

WHAT YOU COULD SAY

'For my next con . . . er, I mean, miracle, I need a pack of cards. As I spread the cards, I'd like you to name any card you see.' (Let him name a card, for example, the King of Diamonds. Take it out of the pack putting it on top of the sticky-faced Three). 'You probably don't know this, but cards have personalities. It's true! In fact the King of Diamonds is actually very shy; if we put him in the limelight he gets very embarrassed. Watch!' (Put the two cards as one on the table, and show the backs of the pack). 'You see, the pack is blue-backed, but the King has got so embarrassed he's blushing!' (Turn the King over showing the red back).

YOU'RE STILL NOT PLAYING WITH A FULL DECK

Let a spectator cut your stacked deck as many times as he likes. Spread the cards face-up, remarking that the pack is completely mixed up (you fibber!) As you do this, look for a 2, any 2, and cut the cards at this point, making sure the 2 goes to the BOTTOM of the pack. From the top of the deck, deal four cards, one to each of the three spectators, the final one to you. Keep doing this in rotation until you each have five cards. If you're a card player, you'll know that this is a POKER DEAL. Ask the first spectator to turn over his cards. He'll be amazed to find he has what is known as a 'straight flush' 1 . Ask the second and third spectators to turn over their cards 2 – they too will have straight Poker flushes. Turn over your cards, remarking that the dealer always wins, showing that you have the best Poker hand of all, a Royal Flush! 3

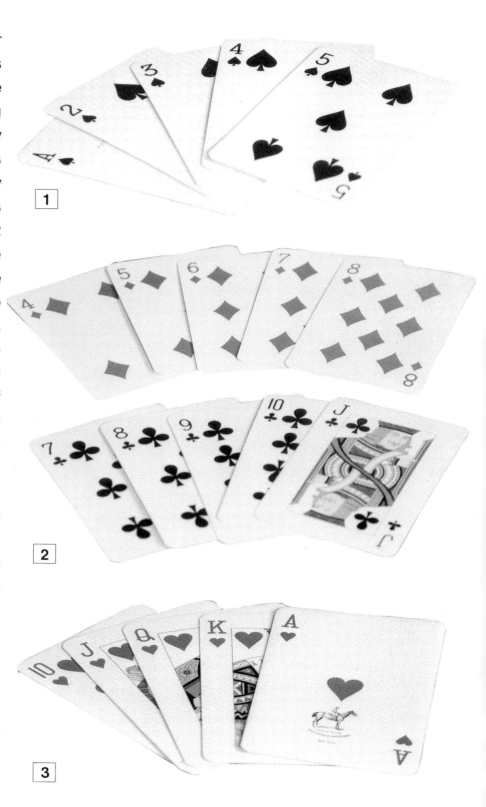

1

2

3

YOU'RE MENTAL!

No, I'm not being rude. 'Mentalism' is, quite simply, magic of the mind. Here are a couple of 'Mental' tricks.

IN THE NEWS

The world's best magician (er . . . that's you), holds up a column of newsprint cut from a newspaper. Holding a pair of scissors, you move your hand along the paper. A spectator calls 'stop' at any time and you cut the newspaper in half at this point. The spectator reads the line of print, at the point where it's been cut. He then opens an envelope which he has held throughout the trick – inside is a piece of paper and on it is the randomly chosen line of print which you have correctly predicted.

HOW IT'S DONE

This is incredibly easy. Cut a column of print from a newspaper, but make sure you cut it a few lines from the top as shown in the picture. Make sure the column doesn't contain any distinguishing features for example, a headline or a wig advert. Now, write the top line of this column on a piece of paper, put it into an envelope and hand this to a spectator before the trick. Hold the newspaper *upside down* and, starting at the top, move the scissors slowly down the paper. If the audience isn't sitting too close, they won't notice that the paper is upside down. Ask a spectator to call 'stop' and at this point cut the paper in half, letting the bottom half flutter to the floor. When he picks this up he will read your original top line, the one you predicted!

WHAT YOU COULD SAY

'I'd like you, Sir, to look after this envelope. Here's a column of newspaper . . .' (Pretend to read from it). 'Oh it says here that police in Blackpool are looking for a man with one eye called Murphy. I wonder what his other eye's called? Sir, as I move the scissors down the newspaper, I'd like you to tell me where to stop. Pick up the piece on the floor and read the top line of newsprint out loud. That was the line you told me to stop at. Please open the envelope. Inside there is a prediction . . . what does it say? Well they've said I'm mental, that proves it!'

THE INCREDIBLE MAGIC SQUARE

You ask someone for a number between 50 and 100. You then draw a square on a piece of paper and divide this into 16 little squares. You write a number inside each of the squares. Each row of numbers adds up to the spectator's number – vertically, diagonally and horizontally. Also the four corner numbers, the four centre squares, any block of four squares.

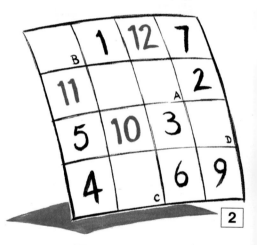

HOW IT'S DONE

OK, you'll need a calculator, an Oxford-educated Professor, a 60 mega-byte computer and . . . no, just kidding! All you really need is a pen and paper. Draw a square on the paper and divide it up into 16 as shown in 1 . Ask for any number between 50 and 100. Write the numbers one to nine in the squares shown in 1. You'll see that each set of two numbers going down vertically add up to nine. An easy way to remember that the six goes next to the nine is to think of the six as an 'upside-down' nine. You then add the numbers 10, 11 and 12 in the positions shown in 2 . You put the numbers one to 12 in these positions every time you

present the 'Magic Square' regardless of the spectator's chosen number. You're now left with four spaces to fill. Subtract 21 from the spectator's chosen number – for example, if the number is 60, subtract 21 giving 39. You're now going to use the number you've arrived at (39 in this example) and the three numbers after it – 40, 41 and 42. Put 39 in the 'A' square 2, 40 in the 'B' square, 41 in the 'C' square and 42 in the 'D' square. You now have your magic square 3 . You'll find that almost every combination of four numbers will add up to their chosen number – vertical, horizontal and diagonal rows, the corners, the centre four squares and any block of four squares.

Magic Square for '60'

▌LET'S HAVE A PARTY!

▌love party magic. And I love practical jokes. Some of the following tricks combine magic with a practical joke, others are ideal for a party situation. With tricks like these, you'll always be the centre of attention!

IT'S UNDER THAT CUP

This is a good one for a party. You turn your back and an object is placed under one of three cups. The cups that the object isn't under are moved around. Yet when you turn back you immediatelly tell your audience where the object is. Mmmmm . . . .

HOW IT'S DONE

Turn three cups mouth downwards and put them on the table. Pick a cup and study the base of it for any distinguishing features. It may have a stain, a chip or a crack. You'll find that every cup has some sort of mark which makes it instantly recognisable. Remember the position of your 'marked' cup. Turn your back and ask a member of the audience to place a coin under any of the three cups. Now ask the spectator to swop the other two cups around. Turn around and look at the position of your 'marked' cup. If the marked cup has been moved, then the coin can't be under it, and it can't be in the place where the marked cup was originally, if you see what I mean! That means that it's under the only other cup. And if the marked cup *hasn't* been moved then the coin must be under it. Let me give you an example. If your marked cup was in the middle and, when you turn round, it is now on the right, you know the coin cannot be under it because it's been moved. You also know that the coin cannot be in the centre position, as that's where the marked cup was originally. Soooooo, it must be under the cup on your left.

WHAT YOU COULD SAY

'I'll bet you this 50p that no matter which cup you hide it under, I'll find it straight away . . . I'll turn my back. Put the 50p under any cup. Now swop the other two cups around. The 50p is under this cup!'

THE THREE BEARS

You'll get some great laughs with this. Soak a little wad of tissue paper in water. Squeeze out the excess fluid until the tissue is just soggy. Conceal the tissue in the fingers of your right hand. Ask a lady to hold out her hand as in the photograph. Place three matches between her fingers as shown. Point to each match in turn as you say, 'This is Daddy Bear, this is Mummy Bear and this is Baby Bear. They were all fast asleep when Daddy Bear woke up at about seven o'clock in the morning. He went into the bathroom.' Take the first match and move it up to the lady's wrist. This represents the bathroom. (You need a good imagination for this!) 'Daddy Bear stayed in the bathroom for a whole hour. As soon as he came out, Mummy Bear got up and went into the bathroom. She was there for nearly two hours.' Move the match back to its original position and take another match, moving it up the wrist as

before. 'Mummy Bear came out of the bathroom and went back to bed.' Move the match back to its original position. 'It was then that Baby Bear got up to go to the bathroom.' Take the third match, and move this towards the wrist as before. Hold the wad of concealed tissue against the match. 'He dashed across the landing, but just before he got to the bathroom, do you know what happened?' Press the paper against the match and water will trickle from the match onto the lady's wrist. From past experience, the lady will inevitably scream!

'. . . Well three hours *is* a long time for a Baby Bear to wait for the bathroom!'

CHUCKLE BOX

'We were so poor . . . Mum used to paint our feet brown and lace up our toes!'

'Where are you from Sir? Good memory!'

33

THE RISING RING

A borrowed finger ring magically floats up a broken rubber band – and everything can be examined by the audience.

HOW IT'S DONE

Snap a thin rubber band so that it becomes one long piece. Hold the band between your hands as in 1 making sure that most of the band is hidden in your right hand. Thread the ring onto the end of the band and stretch it between your fingers as in 2 . OK? By relaxing the pressure of your right finger and thumb, let the hidden section of band slowly slip through your fingers, *keeping your hands perfectly still*. The ring will move with the band, eerily wiggling from one end to the other 3 . Stop when you have let most of the hidden section of band slip through your fingers. This really is quite amazing. Try it!

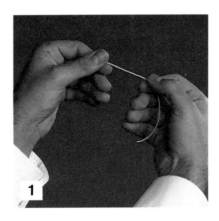

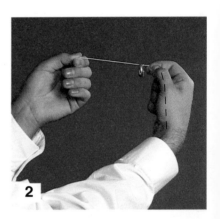

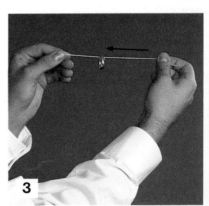

THE SLOT MACHINE SWINDLE

I'll never forget the night some friends and I did this in a hotel. Make no mistake about it, gambling on slot machines is bad news. They take all your money. Some poor guy was pumping money into one of these machines. When he'd run out of money he trudged away, not having won anything. I walked over to the machine with about 50 10p pieces held in my left hand. I pressed a button on the machine then let the money cascade all over the floor. It looked as if they had fallen out of the machine and, as I jubilantly picked up the money, the look on the poor fella's face was a picture! Try this and I bet when you've picked up the money it won't be long before someone else dashes over to have a go!

CHUCKLE BOX

If a few people arrive late: 'You're late . . . was the cinema shut?'

When introducing yourself to someone: 'Have we met before? No? Well how do you know it's me?'

If your assistant is very tall: 'Were you born in a greenhouse?'

OUCH!

The mad magician (yes, you!) throws a hanky over his thumb. Without hesitation he pushes pins through the hanky and through his thumb! The pins are pulled out, the hanky removed, and his thumb looks as healthy as before.

HOW IT'S DONE

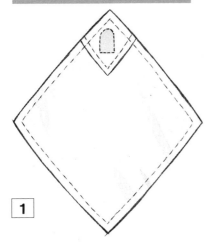

1

You'll need a box of plasters, antiseptic cream and a doctor. No, only kidding! What you will need are two handkerchiefs, some large pins (be careful there!) and one of those rubber 'thingys' called 'finger cones' or rubber thimbles which they use for counting money in banks. Cut a corner from one of the handkerchiefs and sew it onto the other one putting the thimble inside this pocket. To do the trick, hold the hanky by the 'rubber' corner. Drape it over your left hand which has its thumb extended in a 'thumbs up' gesture. As you adjust the hanky with your right hand, push the rubber corner up towards your left thumb. Grasp the base of the thimble with your fingers as shown in **2** . To the audience, it looks as if your

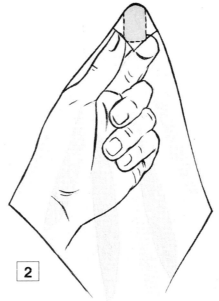

2

thumb is still sticking up, but it's really the thimble. All that's left now is to stick the pins into the thimble as shown in **3** , at the same time giving an 'Oscar-winning performance' with the pained expressions on your face! Remove the pins and grab a corner of the hanky, flicking it off your hand. As you do this, stick your left thumb back into its original position. Show the hanky on both sides and put it in your pocket.

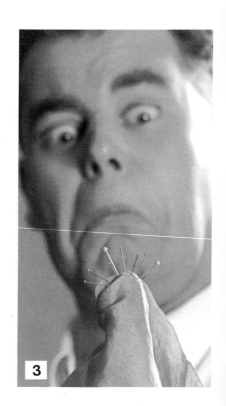

3

SQUEAK! SQUEAK!

Joke and toy shops sell a wonderful thing called 'The Swiss Bird Warbler' which is shown in the picture. They only cost a few pence, but the fun you can get out of them is worth thousands. You put one in your mouth and sort of 'hiss'. It makes a high-pitched 'squeaking' sound and, with practice, you can vary the tone and pitch. Because it's so thin you can actually talk with one still in your mouth. Here's a few gags with the warbler that I regularly do. I'm sure you'll soon be thinking of your own.

1 As you're walking through a busy place, make a little squeaking sound as you put each foot down. People will stare at you. Suddenly stop, look embarrassed, have a look at your shoes and continue walking, squeaking as you go. You'll get some startled and puzzled expressions from onlookers.

2 This is similar to the last gag. But this time you make *someone else's* shoes squeak. As they're walking along, walk nearby making the squeaky noise as the 'victim' puts each foot down. Your victim will look acutely embarrassed. I once had a guy sit down for 20 minutes examining his shoes after I'd played this trick on him!

3 This is a good one to do when you're standing in a lift. Stick one finger in your ear and wiggle it, at the same time making a couple of squeaks. Need I say that you'll get some very funny looks from the people around you.

4 Make your head squeak as you scratch it.

5 Prod a friend in the stomach and make it squeak. Ask him what he ate for breakfast!

6 This is my favourite. All you need is a carrier bag with something inside it. You're walking along when suddenly, little squeaks are heard coming from inside the bag. You whisper gently into the bag, telling the 'animal' to keep quiet. But it gets louder. So you give the bag a few light slaps with your hand. But still it gets louder. You make the bag wriggle and move. The noise finally stops when you give the bag an almighty 'crack' with one hand, then walk off as if nothing had happened. One word of warning though, don't be too good at this or you'll have the RSPCA knocking on your door!

CHUCKLE BOX

'You're a great audience . . . wish I had a better act, really!'

'After this next trick, many people have been heard to ask, "So what?"'

THE DRINKS PROMOTION

This is my favourite party trick. Accompanied with the patter I give later, you'll find it hard to beat. You're seated in a bar or a café and pick up a randomly-chosen beer mat. You tear it in the centre and, from inside the mat you pull a real £5 note. Pass me another beer mat will you!

HOW IT'S DONE

You need to be in a place where they have those cardboard beer or drink mats. Have a banknote folded up very small and palm this in your right hand as in 1 . Pick up a mat with your left hand, show it both sides, and then transfer it to your right hand putting it *over* the note 2 . Show both sides of the mat again, keeping your fingers over the note, so the audience can't see it. Fold the mat in half by bending it under your hand 3 . If you pull your right hand away from the mat, the note will be trapped between the folds. Both hands will now be empty and you can casually show the mat on both sides again, as the note is hidden inside the mat. Fold the mat into quarters. Now, pick at the mat where the note is hidden, separating the layers of the mat, until the note comes into view. It looks as if the note is actually coming from *inside* the layers of cardboard. Eventually, pull the note from inside the mat 4 , open it out, examine it, and put it into your pocket. A spectator will always grab the mat and examine it but, as the layers have been separated, it will look as if the note really has come from inside the mat. It's very important to do this trick casually, as if you've just struck lucky. Believe me, before long the whole place will be in uproar with torn beer mats scattered around the tables as people try to be as lucky as you!

1

4

2

3

WHAT YOU COULD SAY

(Glance at the mats on the table then launch into this, as convincingly as you can!) 'Oh, it's those mats I heard about the other day. Did you know that as a new promotion this drinks company is sealing a £5 note inside one of every 5000 beer mats made. Pass me a mat would you?' (Let a spectator hand you a mat, and fold it up, hiding the £5 inside. Start picking away at the cardboard). 'Yes, you see you just have to tear it in the middle like . . . hang on, look at that . . . I think I've got one!' (Pull out the £5 and open it out). 'Yep! That's real all right. I don't believe it!' (Just you watch the people around you go for all the other mats!)

CHUCKLE BOX

If a trick goes wrong: 'Does anybody want to buy a good trick?'

A closing remark: 'I must go now. I've got another booking . . . next March.'

When handing a pack of cards to a spectator: 'Shuffle them, but don't mix them up.'

If only a couple of people clap: 'Thank you . . . both of you!'

STICKY KNIFE

A knife is magically suspended from your fingers. Aha! But the audience can see how it's done – you're holding it up with your other hand. But when you take your hand away, the knife remains 'magnetized' to your fingers. Golly gosh!

HOW IT'S DONE

Make sure you're wearing a wrist watch. Slip a pencil underneath the strap as in 1 . Keep this hidden up your sleeve. To present the trick, hold the knife in your clenched left fist. Bring your right hand around your wrist and as you open the fingers of your left hand, stretch the forefinger of your right out to press the knife against your hand 2 . Keep the back of your left hand towards the audience, and from the front it will look as if the knife is stuck to your fingers. Hold your hands in this position for a few moments 3 , then turn your hand over so they can see how it's done. Offer to do the trick again. Repeat all the previous movements, but this time,

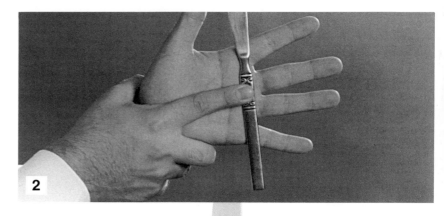

3

complete the trick, pull the knife away from the pencil and toss it on the table. As the audience goes to examine it, push the pencil back up your sleeve or, if you're seated at a table, let it drop out of sight onto your lap.

extend the pencil from out of your left sleeve with your right hand. By pressing the knife against the pencil with your left hand as in **4** it will appear, from the front, as if the knife is magnetized against your fingers. To

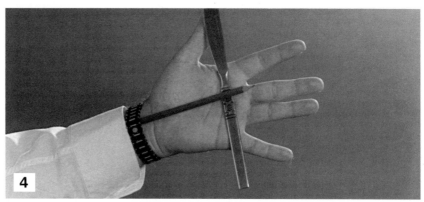

4

CHUCKLE BOX

When handing a pack of cards to a spectator: 'Shuffle them, but don't mix them up.'

If someone is wearing ridiculous clothing: 'Isn't it amazing what you can do with a shower curtain!'

If someone takes your picture during the show: 'I'll have two copies and an enlargement!'

WHAT YOU COULD SAY

'An experiment in mind over matter.' (Suspend the knife as in **2**). 'I don't mind and you don't matter! There are many great feats in the magic world today . . .' (Show them how it's done). 'But this isn't one of them! I'll try again.' (Attach the knife with the pencil, but hold the right hand as before as in pic **2**). 'Doesn't that deserve a round of applause?' (With this, bring your right hand away from left in an applause type gesture, then look quizzically at the knife as it hangs, suspended from your fingers). 'How did I do that?' (Toss the knife onto the table, looking as bewildered as the audience).

IT'S CABARET TIME

Cabaret tricks are ideal for performing in front of a larger audience, although you can still use them in more intimate situations. As there are more people involved, you have to take particular care over your presentation. You must look, move and speak well, ensuring that you keep everyone in the audience interested in what you're doing. You'll probably need some sort of small table and somewhere to keep your tricks. You could design and make a table yourself, allowing space on shelves at the back for the tricks. Or you could rest a briefcase on top of a table, using the case as a table surface, but opening it to get at, and get rid of, your magic.

RABBIT FROM A HAT

This famous trick is rarely seen nowadays, even though it's the trademark of a magician.

HOW IT'S DONE

You'll need a hat, a chair with a solid back, a rabbit and a rabbit bag. The rabbit bag is made from two pieces of material as shown in 1 . Sew it as shown in the diagram, making a hole in one side and sewing an eyelet into the hole to stop the edges from fraying. To the top corner attach a catgut loop which will slip through the hole. The rabbit sits in the bag as in 2 with his paws inside. The bag is held together by

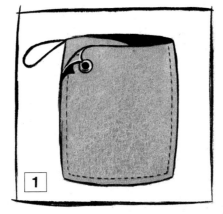

the catgut loop, and this hangs from a nail about 10 cm (4 in) down from the back of the chair. Make sure that the bag is made especially for the rabbit you're using, and that the rabbit is comfortable. You'll find that

with the greatest of respect and never, ever use them in tricks where they may be uncomfortable or in danger. Back to the trick. The bag is now hanging by a nail from the back of the chair, hidden from view. The hat is in your right hand. Ask a member of the audience to the stage to assist you. Hand him the hat and let him examine it. Now offer him a seat and, as you're helping him sit down with your left hand, take the hat in your right. Pass the hat behind the chair, scooping the rabbit and bag up and off the nail and into the hat. Timing here is crucial. You must do this as the person is sitting down, so that his body covers the sneaky moves. The rabbit bag will now automatically open. Hand the hat to your assistant and watch his eyes as a live rabbit peers out!

your rabbit will sit quite happily like this, but don't leave him in the bag too long. The best rabbit to use is a Netherland Dwarf. They are smaller than other breeds and easier to handle. Always remember to treat animals

CHUCKLE BOX

If no-one claps for one of your tricks: 'I once did this for an audience of sheep and they had to count each other to stay awake!

If people are walking across in front of you: 'What's this? A sponsored walk?'

GIVE ME A RING, THAT'S THE KEY

A borrowed finger ring disappears from a glass, only to be found inside your key case, hanging from a clip. The peculiar thing is that the key case has been in full view throughout the trick!

1

HOW IT'S DONE

For years magicians have been making borrowed rings 'fly' into their key cases. Here is a simple but effective way of performing this classic trick. You'll need a leather-type key case like the one shown in 1 . It's important that the case is of the 'snap-shut' variety – don't get one with a zip. You will also need a glass. Bend one of the clips open so that a finger ring will easily slip onto it 2 . Attach a couple of keys to the other clips and close the case, letting the

open clip hang outside the case 3 . Slip this into your pocket. Make up a trick handkerchief like the one used in 'That's Amazing' (page 18), but this time attach a ring to the thread instead of a coin. Borrow a

2

finger ring from a member of the audience. Put the ring underneath the hanky, secretly palming it away as a spectator holds the 'thread ring' through the material (see 'That's Amazing'). Put your hand (which secretly holds the ring) into your pocket and attach the ring to the open clip. Bring the case out of your pocket 4 , concealing the clip and ring behind your hand. Ask the spectator to hold the hanky over the glass (as in 'That's

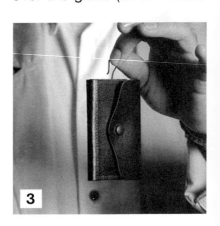

3

CHUCKLE BOX

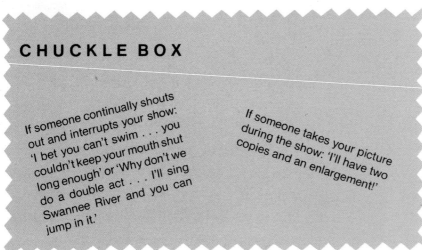

If someone continually shouts out and interrupts your show: 'I bet you can't swim . . . you couldn't keep your mouth shut long enough' or 'Why don't we do a double act . . . I'll sing Swannee River and you can jump in it.'

If someone takes your picture during the show: 'I'll have two copies and an enlargement!'

4

Amazing') and to drop the ring inside. Whip the hand-kerchief away and ask her to take the ring out of the glass. As she's trying to find the ring, put the hanky into your pocket. When she can't find it, open the key case in the position shown in **5** . The keys will fall down on the clips and hang beside the ring. Let the audience see

5

the ring hanging from the clip. Hand the ring to your assistant, asking them to verify that it is theirs. And there you have it. A very simple routine, but one which will have people talking for months to come.

WHAT YOU COULD SAY

'This next trick is best done in front of a live audience, but you'll do until they get here . . . only joking! I'd like to borrow a ring. Thank you Madam. Is this a wedding ring? You've heard of the three rings of marriage haven't you? There's the engagement ring, then the wedding ring and then the suffer-ring! No, it's a lovely ring. Look, there's even a place for the stone! I'll put it under this hanky. Madam, can you feel it through the hanky? Don't let go of the ring – we don't want to lose it. But don't worry, if we do lose your ring you can have the key to my house – it's inside this key case. Hold the hanky over the glass. OK, drop the ring into the glass; now I'd like you to just check that it is actually your ring inside the glass. Pardon? It's gone? What do you mean it's gone? But you were just holding it . . . er, well I've got to go now ladies and gentlemen, you've been a great audience and . . . well, I did say I'd let you have the key to my house if we lost your ring. Here's my key case . . . But look at that – firmly attached to one of the clips is a ring! Now if this ring is your ring then I'm sure the audience will go absolutely wild with applause. Tell us, is that your ring?' (The audience will go wild with applause – we hope!)

THE EGG AND THE HANKY – 'I'LL SHOW YOU HOW IT'S DONE'

I love this trick. It's so simple yet the effect on an audience is astounding. First, you show the audience the famous 'Changing a Hanky Into an Egg Trick'. After you've presented it, you show them how it's done – the egg is hollow and the hanky fits inside it. However, the audience get totally confused when you break the egg into a glass – a real yolk drops out with no sign of the handkerchief!

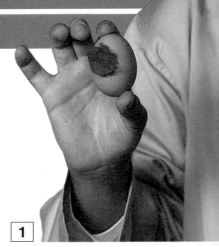

HOW IT'S DONE

You'll need a real egg, a glass, some double-sided sticky tape and a couple of hankies. Take one of the hankies and cut a little scrap of material from it – about 4 cm × 4 cm (1.5 × 1.5 in). Bunch this up and stick it to the egg as shown in 1 . It should look as if a corner of the hanky is protruding from a 'hole' in the egg. The illusion should look perfect, just fiddle about with it until

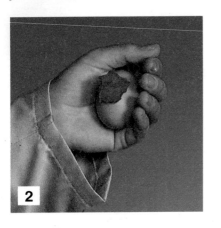

it looks convincing. To present the trick, have a hanky in your right pocket, and the glass on your table. Conceal the egg in your left hand 2 . Take the hanky out of your pocket and give it

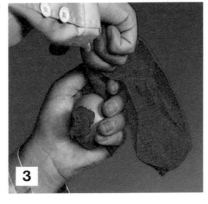

a little shake. With the back of your left hand towards the audience, push the hanky *behind* the egg 3 . When all the hanky has been pushed into your hand, pull the egg away with your right

hand, leaving the hanky behind in your left 4 . Drop your left hand with the concealed hanky casually to your side. Show that the handkerchief has changed into an egg. Offer to show them how it's done. Turn the egg around to reveal the fake hanky. It appears as it there's a hole in the egg and that the hanky is emerging from inside. You can use your left hand to help turn the egg around, but make sure the concealed hanky is not seen by the audience. Explain that the egg is hollow and that the hanky is

5

low and that the hanky is pushed through a hole in the side. Put the egg back into your left hand and *over* the concealed hanky. Pull the hanky out from behind the egg **5** , as if you're pulling it from inside a hollow egg. Display the hanky and repeat the first moves as if you were doing the trick again. However, as you

push the hanky back behind the egg, pull the piece of material away from the sticky tape and push this behind the egg too. Take the egg away in your right hand, with the hanky secretly palmed in your left. Put your left hand into your pocket to get some invisible 'woofle

dust' and leave the hanky behind. Sprinkle the 'dust' over the egg and then break the egg open into the glass as in **6** . If you've presented this trick convincingly you'll get some gasps from the audience, along with some guaranteed applause.

6

WHAT YOU COULD SAY

'Ladies and Gentlemen, brought to you at *enormous* expense, the *world famous handkerchief to egg trick!*' (Throw your right arm out as if expecting applause and then look a little embarrassed). 'Thank you for that sitting ovation . . . Here's the hanky, we push it into the fist and hey presto, it changes into . . . an egg! Look, I'll show you how it's done; you see, the egg is hollow. The yolk has been blown out and there's a hole in the back. To do the trick, take the hanky and keep the egg hidden in your hand. Push the hanky inside the egg and when it's all the way in, you can proudly produce . . . the egg. But if you were a *real* magician you'd prove that this was a real trick. And to do that you'd have to prove that this was a real egg. And the best way to do that is to sprinkle some woofle dust . . . over the top and break it into a glass. Like this!'

WHICH IS THE WAY TO THE SHOW?

To a fast and funny story, the arrows on a sign keep changing direction, resulting in you and the audience becoming completely confused.

Front

1

Back

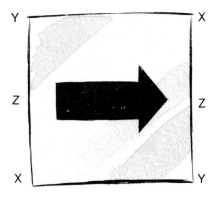

HOW IT'S DONE

This is a good trick to open your cabaret act with. Get some stiff card and cut a 25 cm × 25 cm (10 in × 10 in) square piece from it. Paint or draw an arrow on each side as in 1 . The dotted line shows the position of the arrow on the other side. Hold the card at the points marked 'X' 2 and 3 . Using the fingers of each hand, pivot the card over to show the other side. It will appear as if both arrows are pointing to your left. Do this quickly, three or four times as you're talking. Change position, holding the card at the points marked 'Y' 2 and 4 . If you pivot the card over now, the arrows are pointing in opposite directions. Keeping the hands in the same position, turn the card over two more times. The arrow will now be pointing to *your* right. Move your hands over to the other two

opposite corners and turn the card over 5 . It will appear that both arrows are now pointing to your right. Turn the card over another two times. Change your hand positions to the other two corners again and turn the card over. The arrows will now be pointing in opposites directions. Turn the card over another two times. The arrow facing the audi-

3

4

5

6

ence will now be pointing to your left and the arrow facing you will be pointing upwards. Hold the card at points 'Z' **2** and then turn it over. The arrow will point downwards. Turn it again, it points to the left. Now, turn the card clockwise to your right until the arrow on the front is pointing upwards.

Hold the card as in **6**, and turn it over. It will look as if both arrows are pointing upwards. Turn it over a few more times. Change your hand position to the other two opposite corners and turn the card over. The arrow will now point south. I know all this talk of left and right and 'X, Y and Z' sounds

complicated. Just follow it through step by step and you'll soon get the hang of it.

WHAT YOU COULD SAY

This should all be said very quickly. It doesn't really make any sense, but this, coupled with the arrows continually changing direction, make the trick entertaining. Present it as if you don't really know what's going on yourself and that you're as confused as everyone else. 'I'm sorry I'm a bit late, but I got lost. You see I followed the signs which said go left.' (Holding the card at the points marked X). '. . . but I lost my way. So I asked a tramp if he could direct me. He said, "'Ere, I haven't had a bite for three days". So I bit him. I came to another sign which pointed left, but left was wrong so I went right.' (Pivot the card). 'But that turned out to be wrong – one side was pointing right and one side was pointing left . . . right?' (Turn the card over twice). 'I saw another sign – that was pointing right on both sides so it must have been right.' (Turn the card over). 'But I got really confused when they pointed left *and* right.' (Turn the card over again). 'I didn't know which way to turn.' (Turn the card twice). 'So I thought I'd go south . . .' (Hold the card at the Zs and turn it so that the arrow points downwards. Turn it again so that it points left). '. . . instead of left. But that didn't work so I went north.' (Turn the card clockwise). 'Until I ended up in John O'Groats . . .' (Hold the card as in **6** and turn it over). 'John said, "You've got it wrong – left's wrong, right's wrong, north's wrong, south's right." So he put me in a taxi and sent me south, and that's why I'm late. And if you believe that, you can knit wire netting.' (A silly gag to wind the trick up – toss the card aside and launch into your next trick).

I'LL START AGAIN

As you go through a funny patter routine you count the six cards which you hold in your hand. You then throw three away ... but you still have six cards. You throw another three cards away but *still* you have six cards. This happens several times as the trick works up to an even more puzzling climax.

HOW IT'S DONE

'Buckle Count'. That doesn't mean much to you does it? It's the magicians' term for a special way of counting the cards. You can make 10, 20 or 30 cards look like only six, although the more cards you are holding the harder it is.

Hold 18 cards in your left hand as in 1 . You're going to count them as six cards. Push off four cards, one at a time, into your right hand 2 taking each card *under* the one before it. When it comes to the fifth card, bend your left fingers

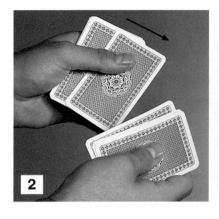

inwards and 'buckle' the bottom card as in 3 . Now take all the cards above this bottom one, away in your right hand 4 . Hold them together in one block as if they were one card. Count the last card as number six. The first time you do this you'll probably feel very uncomfortable. Don't worry. Practise until you can do it smoothly – it won't take long. Your timing here is so important. It should be 'one, two, three, four, five, six' and *not* 'one, two, three, four, . . . five, six.' Throw three cards away,

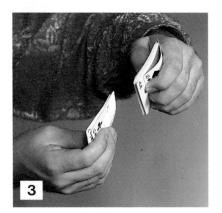

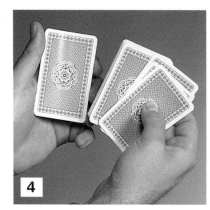

one at a time, and then count the cards as six again. This move is repeated throughout the trick. When you're counting, hold the cards in the position shown in 5 . When you throw each card away, throw it up and into the air, letting it flutter to the floor. This makes the pre-sentation so much more impressive and 'showy'. The patter for this trick 'makes' it. I'll tell you when to do the count as I run through the chatter.

WHAT YOU COULD SAY

(Hold 18 cards in your left hand). 'The other day I saw a magician and he did a trick where he had one, two, three, four, five, six cards . . .' (Count the 18 as six). 'He threw one, two, three away.' (Throw three cards away). 'But he still had one, two, three, four, five, six cards left.' (Pause). 'Well I thought it was a great trick, so after the show I went to see him. I said, "That was a great trick you did." He said, "What trick was that?" I said, "The one where you take one, two, three, four, five, six cards." (Count the now 15 cards as six). "You throw one, two, three cards away." (Throw three away). ". . . But you still have one, two, three, four, five, six cards left." ' (Count the 12 cards as six). 'He said, "Oh you mean the trick where you take six cards and you throw one, two, three away." (Throw three cards away). "But you still have one, two, three, four, five, six cards left." ' (Count the nine cards as six). 'I said, "Yes! How do you do it?" Well he showed me, so tonight I'm going to show *you* the incredible trick where you take one, two, three, four, five, six cards.' (Count the nine as six again). 'You throw one, two, three cards away.' (Throw three away). '*But* you still have one, two . . . three cards?' (This time count the remaining six cards as three and look puzzled as the trick has apparently gone wrong. Pause for a few moments, the audience will probably laugh). 'You know, when the magician did it he had one, two, three, four, five, six cards left!' (Throw the six cards in your hand into the air one at a time and wait for the applause).

THIS IS ROPEY!

There's an old saying, 'Give a magician enough rope and he'll show you a trick.' You can use any soft and supple cotton rope. If you can't find any then magic dealers sell rope made for magicians. Here's a couple of my favourite rope tricks.

THE FAIRLY AMAZING ROPE TRICK

A piece of rope is cut into two pieces. They are tied together. You then slide the knot off the end of the rope, so that you're holding a knot in one hand and a complete piece of rope in the other. That was good, wasn't it?

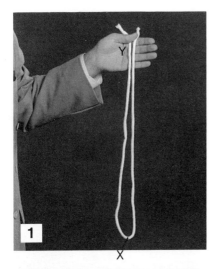

HOW IT'S DONE

For this trick, all you need are a pair of scissors and a piece of rope about a metre (3 ft 6 in) long. Hold the rope in your left hand as in 1 . Grab the middle of the rope at the point marked 'X' and bring it up towards your left hand. Under cover of the left hand, take the rope at the point marked 'Y' as shown in 2 and put this loop of rope under your left thumb 3 . Seen from the front, it looks as if you've just brought the centre of the rope up into your left hand. Ask someone to cut through this loop with the scissors as in 4 . Let the long ends drop down so that you are holding two loops of rope 5 . Keep your thumb over the join and it will look like two separate pieces of rope. Now, tie the small loop around the rope, as if you are tying the two pieces together. Pull it tight. It will

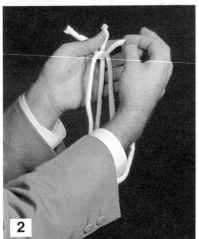

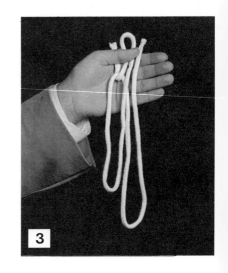

your right hand, slide the knot slowly off the end of the rope. Toss the knot and the restored rope to the spectators for examination and take your well-deserved bow!

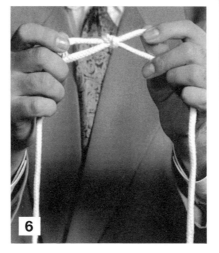

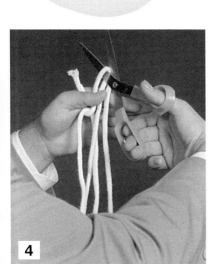

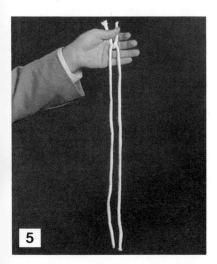

look as if the two pieces are knotted together, whereas you've simply tied the short loop around the long one. Tell your audience that you're going to make the knot disappear. Give the rope a shake and quickly move your right hand over the knot. They won't be very impressed. Offer to bring the knot back, shake the rope and take your right hand away. Everyone will look at you as if you're crackers! With the fingers of

WHAT YOU COULD SAY

'A trick with a piece of string. Well, it was a piece of string but I've been feeding it on *Shredded Wheat*. A quick impression – a continent.' (Hold the rope in a 'U' shape). 'There you are . . . "U" rope . . . Europe. Get it?' (Don't dwell too long on this joke, it's terrible!) 'Sir, I'd like you to cut the rope in the centre. We'll tie the two ends together. Now, watch the knot, because I'm going to make it disappear. Are you ready? There! Gone! You're not impressed? I'll bring it back, watch – here it is! Are you sure you're watching the knot? Anyone who's watching a knot is knot watching. Tell you what, I'll slide the knot off like this, and you can take it home and watch it!'

SILLY SPAGHETTI

A short length of rope, a medium length of rope and a long length of rope are held up. Slowly and visibly they all become the same size. But with a squeeze of the hand and a little jiggery-pokery they revert back to their original sizes. And all the ropes can be examined.

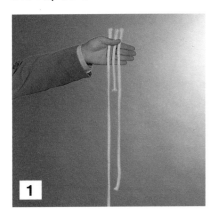

1

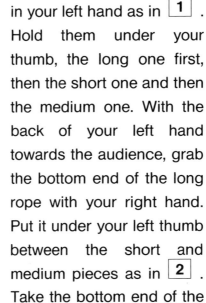

2

3

HOW IT'S DONE

This is a good trick to show children. It's easy to follow and the visible transformation is quite astounding. You will need three lengths of rope – one about 90 cm (35 in) long, another about 50 cm (20 in) long and another 20 cm (8 in) long.

Show the pieces of rope to the audience and put them in your left hand as in 1 . Hold them under your thumb, the long one first, then the short one and then the medium one. With the back of your left hand towards the audience, grab the bottom end of the long rope with your right hand. Put it under your left thumb between the short and medium pieces as in 2 . Take the bottom end of the short piece with your right hand and put this in a position to the left of the medium piece as in 3 . Finally, take the bottom end of the medium piece and put this in the position shown in 4 . I know all that sounds

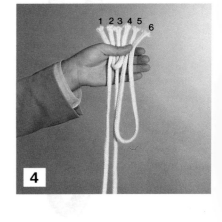

1 2 3 4 5 6

4

complicated. It isn't. It's just very hard to explain! Now, with your right hand, grab ends 1, 4 and 6, keeping ends 2, 3 and 5 in your left hand. Hold the two hands in the position shown in 5 . Move both your hands slowly apart, and it will appear as if the ropes are all becoming the same length. Release the ends from your right hand and hold the

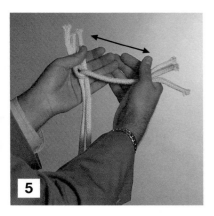

5

6

7

ropes as in **6** keeping your left thumb over the 'loop'. To the audience, the ropes all now appear to be the same length. You're now going to count them. Take the medium rope away in your right hand, counting this as 'one' **7** . Move your right hand back towards your left. Clip the ends of the short piece in your left hand between your right fore and middle fingers. Move these ends away and to the right counting 'two'. At the same time, leave the medium piece behind under your left thumb **8** . Move your right hand back towards your left, taking the medium piece again and counting 'three'. It looks as if you've just counted three single pieces of rope. In actual fact, two are joined together. Practise until you can count them smoothly. It should be 'one, two, three' and *not* 'one . . . two, three'. Bunch the ropes up into your left hand and then pull them out one at a time, showing that they've now reverted back to their original assorted lengths. This is probably one of the most effective rope tricks you can do.

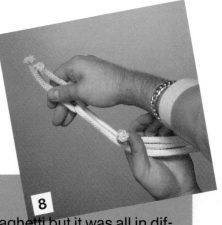

8

WHAT YOU COULD SAY

'A funny thing happened to me the other day. I bought some spaghetti but it was all in different lengths. Some was long, some was medium and some was short.' (Hold the three pieces up for the audience). 'So I took the spaghetti back to the shop. I said "This is no good, I like my spaghetti to be the same length." The shopkeeper, who was Italian, shouted "Mam-am-ee-a." That was because his mum had just walked into the shop. "Mam I'm here," get it? Oh never mind! He took the spaghetti, gathered up the ends,' (gather the ends of the three pieces of rope into your hand) 'and gave a little blow. And the amazing thing is, all the spaghetti became the same length.' (Release the ends). 'Well, he put it back in the packet.' (Count the pieces). 'And I took it home. But I couldn't believe it when I opened the packet . . .' (Pull the pieces, one by one, out of your hand). 'Because all I found was three pieces of spaghetti, one long, one medium and one short. So I had fish and chips instead!'

IT'S NOT JUST TRICKS!

It certainly isn't! There's so many other things to think about. The following pages give you important information about presenting yourself and your tricks effectively, and how to become a professional magician – if you want to.

THE UNWRITTEN RULES

1. *Never tell your audience how your tricks are done.* If you tell them, you'll no longer be able to entertain them will you? Keep them guessing, let them think it's harder than it actually is. If someone asks, 'How do you do it?' just say, 'Brilliantly!'

2. *Practise.* Boy, is this important! Practise, practise, practise. If you get bored, do the trick in front of the dog or the cactus. The best training of all is in front of an audience. Go out and show the trick to as many friends as possible.

3. *Entertain them!* This is the most important rule of all. You're not there to show people how clever you are; you're there to help them have a good time and enjoy your magic. So, don't forget – entertain them!

4. *Never repeat a trick to the same audience.* If you do the same trick again they'll be watching even closer – and all your misdirection will be useless.

5. *Leave 'em wanting more!* This old showbiz expression certainly holds true with magic. Don't go on too long, it's fatal.

6. *If they like you, they'll like the tricks.* Let's face it, most magicians can do most tricks. So the audience are interested in *you* and how you present yourself to them. Smile a lot. A smile transforms a face, bringing it alive. Make sure you look people in the eye. You'll appear more confident and people will feel more involved in your performance. When you do a sneaky move, look directly at them and they won't spot a thing. If you spend all your time looking at the floor you'll only end up making the carpet feel more involved, not the audience. Oh, and don't forget to speak up.

GETTING YOUR ACT TOGETHER!

No matter how long your act is, you need a beginning, a middle and an end. Your opening trick should be quite quick and slick – something you know well. It's a means of letting the audience get to know you. Don't open your act with a trick that requires an assistant, as the focus should be totally on you. Remember, if they like you, they'll like your tricks. The middle of your act should flow smoothly and should keep their interest. Your final trick should be your best – a real 'knock out' that will leave them wanting more. Don't put the same type of tricks together in your act. For example, don't cut and restore a rope and then tear and restore a cigarette paper – it's basically the same trick.

USING A MICROPHONE

If you're performing in front of a lot of people, you'll probably need to use a microphone. Don't be frightened of it. Familiarize yourself with the mike and its stand before you go on. Check whether the mike has an 'on/off' switch and make sure it's 'on' when you start speaking. Have a look at the stand and check that it's stable and won't fall apart during your performance. Practise putting the mike in the stand's clip, without making too much noise. Handle a microphone gently. Don't bang it around as it makes a terrible sound through the speakers. And don't cough into the microphone. Apart from giving the mike a sore throat it sounds like a bomb going off. Hold the mike about 15 cm (6 in) from your mouth. If you hold it too close people won't be able to see your facial expressions. If you're doing a trick which requires the use of both hands, put the mike in the stand's clip and put your arms around the stand so that your hands are in front. You can then turn to the left and right, keeping the mike at the correct distance from your mouth. If you have to move away from the mike, speak louder and it will pick your voice up. One more thing, make sure you know where the microphone cable is, otherwise you may trip over it.

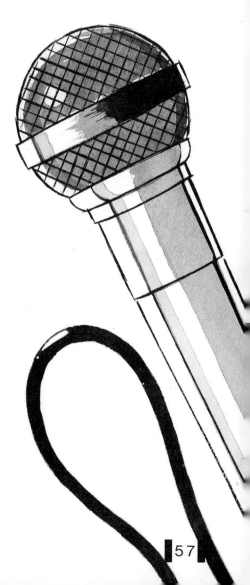

DRESS

Always look smart. Even if you're doing a close-up show in jeans to half a dozen people, make sure you look neat and tidy. If you don't look right the audience will be too busy thinking about your appearance to be watching the tricks. Keep your hands clean, especially your nails, and keep your hair in good condition . . . I'm beginning to sound like your mother, aren't I!

USING COMEDY

Making people laugh is a fabulous feeling. But not everyone can do it. It takes practice. There is no doubt, however, that a magic act can be dramatically improved with a few funny lines and situations along the way. Many of the tricks in this book have some 'comedy patter' attached to them. Most of the gags here are quite corny, but you can easily expand on them. There are some golden rules to remember when delivering comedy.

1 Correct timing. Timing is knowing the speed at which to tell your jokes in a particular situation and delivering the 'tag line' at the right moment. Timing is something that cannot be taught. It only comes with practice. Watch professional comedians carefully, and study how they tell their jokes.

2 Don't speak too fast, or people will miss what you're saying.

3 Don't say your funny line while the audience is clapping or still laughing loudly. They'll miss it.

4 Don't overdo it. Too many jokes will just confuse the magic.

5 If you don't feel comfortable using the odd funny line, don't do it. You can still add lots of humour. For example, in *Give Me A Ring, That's The Key* the fact that you have supposedly lost the spectator's ring is funny in itself. Here, it is the situation that is humorous, not what you are saying. This sort of comedy is called 'situation comedy' and is often the funniest of all.

STAGEFRIGHT

Everyone gets it. I've seen some of the big stars physically shake with fear before they go on stage, so you're not on your own. It's nature's way of telling you that your body is ready for action. Take some deep breaths. Run on the spot. This will get the adrenalin going. Look in a mirror and tell yourself how great you are, and how the audience is about to watch the best entertainer they've ever seen! It works!

STAGECRAFT

This starts with walking out onto the stage. Plaster a big smile on your face and stroll briskly to the spot where you will be performing. A crucial point here is to look the audience in the eye as you walk. Do this by quickly moving your eyes along the rows of people. Everyone will feel as if you've looked at them individually so you will have already established a good rapport. During your act it's important to look at every member of the audience, keeping everyone involved. Try not to turn your back on the audience during your act, and make sure you're saying or doing something all the time. At the climax of a trick, where you want some applause, open your palms towards the audience and pause, looking at them. Stay like that until they clap! They will, I promise. As soon as they start clapping, don't say a thing until they stop. Audiences are strange. As soon as one person claps the rest will follow. At the end of your act, after you've said something like, 'You've been a great audience, goodnight' the audience will start clapping. Take a bow from the waist, keeping your hands clasped gently together in front of your body. As soon as you feel the applause fading, get off quick. You'll look silly if they've stopped clapping and you're still taking a bow.

WHERE CAN YOU DO YOUR ACT?

If you're just starting out, why not try a talent show? They're good for practice. Put on a show for a local charity, or try out your tricks at a local old folks home. Get involved with a local drama group. These sorts of groups put shows on regularly, and it's more than likely that they'll welcome the idea of a magic act to add a bit of variety to the production. Keep in touch with showbusiness by reading theatrical newspapers. As you get better, you could start approaching local hotels or clubs. Take your close-up tricks along to a local restaurant and suggest to the manager that you could show his clients a couple of tricks at their tables. Don't forget that the best sort of practice you can get is in front of a live audience, so do as many shows as you can. As you get better, you'll be able to charge money for your time and, who knows, one day you may decide to turn professional.

GETTING ON TELEVISION

Television loves magic. That's because magic is so visual, and it's a lot more interesting than just interviewing someone. If you're going to do some magic on TV you must stick to tricks that are short and uncomplicated. But how do you get on in the first place? Start with your local television stations. They usually have local magazine programmes which are tailor made for interviews with magicians. But the fact that you're a magician isn't going to get you on there. You have to find what media people call 'an angle'. For example, if you're still at school, but are doing lots of shows, that's a novelty which they would like. Or, if you're a waiter or waitress who does a bit of magic for the customers, that would be a nice story for the cameras to follow. Write to the producers of other suitable programmes. Offer to go on and do a few tricks and ask for an interview. If they say 'no' keep pestering them until they say 'yes'. They'll get so fed up of hearing from you that they'll use you just to keep you quiet!

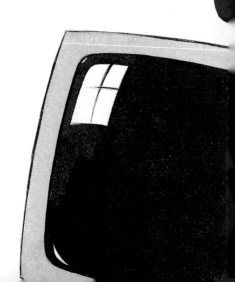

ANY PUBLICITY IS GOOD PUBLICITY

If people don't know about you, how can they book you? You have to let them know you're there. You do this with publicity. A good place to start is your local paper. Get to know a journalist there. I remember I wrote to the local paper when I was about ten, asking if they could help me get a top hat. This they did, running a long article about the story, and following this up with several pieces on my progress with my act. If you can get a paper interested in you, you'll get a mountain of publicity. Write lots of letters to prospective 'bookers'. Let people know that you're there, without appearing to be big-headed or conceited. If you're at a party or a function, do a few tricks. People will start asking you questions, and word will soon spread that you're a magician. If you're taking performing really seriously, you'll probably need some photographs of yourself. Get them done at a good theatrical photographers. If you can't afford that, why not approach a local photographic society who may take them as part of a project. Don't clutter the picture up with props – a good, clear head and shoulders shot is fine. Alternatively, try and make up your own unusual and striking picture – perhaps you're jumping in the air, or you're sitting with your feet up, holding a pack of cards. Once you've got your picture you can have it reproduced on card. Theatrical newspapers have the addresses of people who specialise in this sort of thing. If you have some postcard size reproductions done you can include your telephone number on the back and use them as business cards. Whenever you meet someone who may be able to give you a booking, let them have a photograph. They're more likely to keep hold of this than throw it away. As far as photos, business cards, letterheads and so on are concerned, always get the best you can afford. Quality really does make a difference.

DYING A DEATH

This will happen. You'll go out in front of an audience and get hardly any response. Don't worry about it. Just keep smiling. If you've done the same act elsewhere and the audience loved it, then it's got to be the audience who is bad, not you. Not everyone will like you. Accept that and you'll come out on top.

TURNING PROFESSIONAL

OK, so you've got a good act, you've done plenty of shows, people are prepared to pay well for your time, and you love performing. You'd like to turn professional. Showbusiness is traditionally one of the hardest of the professions to be successful in. But it's also one of the most exciting, fulfilling and rewarding. You must be strong-willed, determined to succeed, prepared to have your confidence knocked time and time again, to go for several weeks without work, and to work at some of the darkest and dingiest places imaginable. Approach as many entertainment agents as possible. There are so many different places that you can work – cruise liners, hotels, theatres, children's parties, clubs, restaurants, business conventions and holiday camps, to name a few. But success doesn't come overnight. It takes time. Remember, a lawyer takes eight years to qualify. Why shouldn't you?

USING MAGIC IN EVERYDAY LIFE

Magic is a fantastic hobby. And it opens many doors. Socially, it's a great asset. Showing a few tricks at a party will draw people to you and you'll make a mountain of new friends. If you're working as a salesman for example, a magic trick can work wonders. If you show your clients a trick every time you see them, they'll actually look forward to seeing you each time, and be more open to listening to the other things you have to say. The same applies if you go for a job interview. Show them a trick and you'll certainly stand out from all the others. If you're travelling abroad, show a few visual tricks to a shopkeeper. Magic has no language barrier, and after a few tricks you'll soon become the centre of attention.

FINAL WORD

I told you at the beginning that your life would change. Well, has it? Thought so. Magic does that to you.

All the very best,

*

*Who?

WITH THANKS

The author would like to thank the many people who have helped him over the years, in particular:

Peter Bailey, Jacqui Morley, 'Little' Harry Dewhirst, Jack Ganley, Michael Vine for the wind-ups and pep-talks, Cyril Critchlowe, Colin Harmer, Tony Clinning, Derek Lever, Doug Olney for the beef sandwich, Grandad for the transport, Christopher Pilkington, Richard Simkin, David Crichton, Dennis Spence for the driving lessons, St. Paul's Sunday School, BBC TV Training, Claremont Primary School, Eileen Skelly for the 26 shows a night, John Lettice, the staff of Warbreck High School Blackpool and the many magicians from whom he has learnt a great deal of the magic.

MAGIC SOCIETIES

Most large towns and cities have a magic club. They usually have a programme of events which will include things such as lectures by top magicians, shows for the public, magic competitions and trips to magic conventions. A couple of the major magic societies are listed below. If you want to find out more, write enclosing a stamped addressed to:

International Brotherhood of Magicians,
Headquarters,
28 North Main Street,
Kenton,
Ohio 43326,
USA.

If you live in the UK, write to:
H. J. Atkins,
Kings Garne,
Fricham Court,
Fricham,
Lyndhurst,
Hampshire,
England.

The Magic Circle,
c/o Christopher Pratt,
The Secretary,
Magic Circle,
13 Calder Avenue,
Brookmans Park,
Hertfordshire,
AL9 7AH,
England.

The Society of American Magicians,
c/o John Apperson,
2812 Idaho,
Granite City,
IL 62040,
USA.

MAGIC SUPPLIERS

Here are a few professional magic dealers. You can usually buy catalogues from them detailing their tricks. Drop them a line, enclosing a stamped addressed envelope to find out more.

Stacey's Magic Palace,
44 Museum Street,
London WC1A 1LY,
England.

The Supreme Magic Company Ltd.,
Supreme House,
Bideford,
Devon,
EX39 2AN,
England.
(This is the largest magic dealer in the world. They also publish a monthly magic magazine.)

International Magic Studio,
89 Clerkenwell Road,
London,
EC1,
England.

The Magic Hands,
Modern Magic Studio,
Postfach G,
D-7033 Herrenberg,
West Germany.

Abbotts Magic Manufacturing Co.,
Colon,
Michigan 49040,
USA.

The world's only weekly magic magazine, *Abracadabra* is published by:
Goodliffe Publications Ltd.,
150 New Road,
Bromsgrove,
Worcestershire,
B60 2LG,
England.